This Planner Belongs To:

_____

Weekly Snapshot

MON:

TUE: Fun & Games
      Lynn's

WED:

THUR:

FRI:

SAT:

SUN:

REMINDERS

TO DO LIST

NOTES

My Action Plan

DATE:

TOP PRIORITIES	GOALS

ACTION STEPS	STATUS	✓

MILESTONES & REWARDS:

THOUGHTS & REFLECTIONS::

Weekly Priority List

March

13
MON

14
TUE

10:00 Fund Games — Lynn's

15
WED

16
THUR

9:30 Infectious Disease
Hillcrest So. DRI Bldg

17
FRI

18
SAT

19
SUN

Checklist

FOR: DATE: ✓

NOTES:

Daily Planner

DATE
_____

TOP PRIORITIES:

APPOINTMENTS:

GOALS FOR THE DAY::

MORNING:

AFTERNOON:

EVENING:

NOTES:

Daily Planner

DATE

_____

MORNING:

TOP PRIORITIES:

AFTERNOON:

EVENING:

APPOINTMENTS:

NOTES:

GOALS FOR THE DAY::

Daily Planner

DATE
_____

TOP PRIORITIES:

APPOINTMENTS:

GOALS FOR THE DAY::

MORNING:

AFTERNOON:

EVENING:

NOTES:

Daily Planner

DATE

TOP PRIORITIES:

APPOINTMENTS:

GOALS FOR THE DAY::

MORNING:

AFTERNOON:

EVENING:

NOTES:

Daily Planner

DATE

_____

TOP PRIORITIES:

APPOINTMENTS:

GOALS FOR THE DAY::

MORNING:

AFTERNOON:

EVENING:

NOTES:

Daily Planner

DATE
_____

TOP PRIORITIES:

APPOINTMENTS:

GOALS FOR THE DAY::

MORNING:

AFTERNOON:

EVENING:

NOTES:

Daily Planner

DATE
_____

TOP PRIORITIES:

APPOINTMENTS:

GOALS FOR THE DAY::

MORNING:

AFTERNOON:

EVENING:

NOTES:

Weekly Snapshot

MON:

TUE:

WED:

THUR:

FRI:

SAT:

SUN:

TO DO LIST

NOTES

REMINDERS

Daily Planner

DATE

_____

TOP PRIORITIES:

APPOINTMENTS:

GOALS FOR THE DAY::

MORNING:

AFTERNOON:

EVENING:

NOTES:

Daily Planner

DATE

_____

TOP PRIORITIES:

APPOINTMENTS:

GOALS FOR THE DAY::

MORNING:

AFTERNOON:

EVENING:

NOTES:

Daily Planner

DATE
_____

TOP PRIORITIES:

APPOINTMENTS:

GOALS FOR THE DAY::

MORNING:

AFTERNOON:

EVENING:

NOTES:

Daily Planner

DATE

_____

TOP PRIORITIES:

APPOINTMENTS:

GOALS FOR THE DAY::

MORNING:

AFTERNOON:

EVENING:

NOTES:

Daily Planner

DATE

_____

TOP PRIORITIES:

APPOINTMENTS:

GOALS FOR THE DAY::

MORNING:

AFTERNOON:

EVENING:

NOTES:

Daily Planner

DATE
_____

TOP PRIORITIES:

APPOINTMENTS:

GOALS FOR THE DAY::

MORNING:

AFTERNOON:

EVENING:

NOTES:

Daily Planner

DATE
_____

TOP PRIORITIES:

APPOINTMENTS:

GOALS FOR THE DAY::

MORNING:

AFTERNOON:

EVENING:

NOTES:

Daily Planner

DATE
_____

TOP PRIORITIES:

MORNING:

AFTERNOON:

EVENING:

APPOINTMENTS:

NOTES:

GOALS FOR THE DAY::

Daily Planner

DATE

_____

TOP PRIORITIES:

APPOINTMENTS:

GOALS FOR THE DAY::

MORNING:

AFTERNOON:

EVENING:

NOTES:

Daily Planner

DATE

_____

TOP PRIORITIES:

MORNING:

AFTERNOON:

EVENING:

APPOINTMENTS:

NOTES:

GOALS FOR THE DAY::

Daily Planner

DATE

_____

TOP PRIORITIES:

APPOINTMENTS:

GOALS FOR THE DAY::

MORNING:

AFTERNOON:

EVENING:

NOTES:

Weekly Snapshot

MON:

TUE:

WED:

THUR:

FRI:

SAT:

SUN:

TO DO LIST

NOTES

REMINDERS

My Action Plan

DATE:

TOP PRIORITIES   GOALS

ACTION STEPS   STATUS   ✓

MILESTONES & REWARDS:

THOUGHTS & REFLECTIONS::

Weekly Priority List

MON	
TUE	
WED	
THUR	
FRI	
SAT	
SUN	

Checklist

FOR: DATE:

NOTES:

Daily Planner

DATE
_____

TOP PRIORITIES:

APPOINTMENTS:

GOALS FOR THE DAY::

MORNING:

AFTERNOON:

EVENING:

NOTES:

Daily Planner

DATE

_____

TOP PRIORITIES:

APPOINTMENTS:

GOALS FOR THE DAY::

MORNING:

AFTERNOON:

EVENING:

NOTES:

Daily Planner

DATE
_____

TOP PRIORITIES:

APPOINTMENTS:

GOALS FOR THE DAY::

MORNING:

AFTERNOON:

EVENING:

NOTES:

Daily Planner

DATE

_____

TOP PRIORITIES:

APPOINTMENTS:

GOALS FOR THE DAY::

MORNING:

AFTERNOON:

EVENING:

NOTES:

Daily Planner

DATE
_____

TOP PRIORITIES:

APPOINTMENTS:

GOALS FOR THE DAY::

MORNING:

AFTERNOON:

EVENING:

NOTES:

Daily Planner

DATE

_____

TOP PRIORITIES:

APPOINTMENTS:

MORNING:

AFTERNOON:

EVENING:

NOTES:

GOALS FOR THE DAY::

Daily Planner

DATE
_____

TOP PRIORITIES:

APPOINTMENTS:

GOALS FOR THE DAY::

MORNING:

AFTERNOON:

EVENING:

NOTES:

Weekly Snapshot

MON:

TUE:

WED:

THUR:

FRI:

SAT:

SUN:

REMINDERS

TO DO LIST

NOTES

My Action Plan

DATE:

TOP PRIORITIES	GOALS

ACTION STEPS	STATUS	✓

MILESTONES & REWARDS:

THOUGHTS & REFLECTIONS::

Weekly Priority List

MON

TUE

WED

THUR

FRI

SAT

SUN

Checklist

FOR: DATE: ✓

NOTES:

Daily Planner

DATE

_____

TOP PRIORITIES:

APPOINTMENTS:

GOALS FOR THE DAY::

MORNING:

AFTERNOON:

EVENING:

NOTES:

Daily Planner

DATE
_____

TOP PRIORITIES:

APPOINTMENTS:

GOALS FOR THE DAY::

MORNING:

AFTERNOON:

EVENING:

NOTES:

Daily Planner

DATE
_____

TOP PRIORITIES:

APPOINTMENTS:

GOALS FOR THE DAY::

MORNING:

AFTERNOON:

EVENING:

NOTES:

Daily Planner

DATE

TOP PRIORITIES:

APPOINTMENTS:

GOALS FOR THE DAY::

MORNING:

AFTERNOON:

EVENING:

NOTES:

Daily Planner

DATE

_____

MORNING:

TOP PRIORITIES:

AFTERNOON:

EVENING:

APPOINTMENTS:

NOTES:

GOALS FOR THE DAY::

Daily Planner

DATE
_____

TOP PRIORITIES:

APPOINTMENTS:

GOALS FOR THE DAY::

MORNING:

AFTERNOON:

EVENING:

NOTES:

Daily Planner

DATE
_____

TOP PRIORITIES:

APPOINTMENTS:

GOALS FOR THE DAY::

MORNING:

AFTERNOON:

EVENING:

NOTES:

Weekly Snapshot

MON:

TUE:

WED:

THUR:

FRI:

SAT:

SUN:

TO DO LIST

NOTES

REMINDERS

My Action Plan

DATE:

TOP PRIORITIES   GOALS

ACTION STEPS   STATUS   ✓

MILESTONES & REWARDS:

THOUGHTS & REFLECTIONS::

Weekly Priority List

MON	
TUE	
WED	
THUR	
FRI	
SAT	
SUN	

Checklist

FOR: DATE:

NOTES:

Daily Planner

DATE
_____

TOP PRIORITIES:

APPOINTMENTS:

GOALS FOR THE DAY::

MORNING:

AFTERNOON:

EVENING:

NOTES:

Daily Planner

DATE

_____

TOP PRIORITIES:

APPOINTMENTS:

GOALS FOR THE DAY::

MORNING:

AFTERNOON:

EVENING:

NOTES:

Daily Planner

DATE

TOP PRIORITIES:

APPOINTMENTS:

GOALS FOR THE DAY::

MORNING:

AFTERNOON:

EVENING:

NOTES:

Daily Planner

DATE
_____

TOP PRIORITIES:

APPOINTMENTS:

GOALS FOR THE DAY::

MORNING:

AFTERNOON:

EVENING:

NOTES:

Daily Planner

DATE
_____

TOP PRIORITIES:

MORNING:

AFTERNOON:

EVENING:

APPOINTMENTS:

NOTES:

GOALS FOR THE DAY::

Daily Planner

DATE
_____

TOP PRIORITIES:

APPOINTMENTS:

GOALS FOR THE DAY::

MORNING:

AFTERNOON:

EVENING:

NOTES:

Daily Planner

DATE

TOP PRIORITIES:

APPOINTMENTS:

GOALS FOR THE DAY::

MORNING:

AFTERNOON:

EVENING:

NOTES:

Weekly Snapshot

MON:

TUE:

WED:

THUR:

FRI:

SAT:

SUN:

REMINDERS

TO DO LIST

NOTES

My Action Plan

DATE:

TOP PRIORITIES

GOALS

ACTION STEPS

STATUS   ✓

MILESTONES & REWARDS:

THOUGHTS & REFLECTIONS::

Weekly Priority List

MON

TUE

WED

THUR

FRI

SAT

SUN

Checklist

FOR: DATE: ✓

NOTES:

Daily Planner

DATE

_____

TOP PRIORITIES:

APPOINTMENTS:

GOALS FOR THE DAY::

MORNING:

AFTERNOON:

EVENING:

NOTES:

Daily Planner

DATE

TOP PRIORITIES:

APPOINTMENTS:

GOALS FOR THE DAY::

MORNING:

AFTERNOON:

EVENING:

NOTES:

Daily Planner

DATE
_____

TOP PRIORITIES:

APPOINTMENTS:

GOALS FOR THE DAY::

MORNING:

AFTERNOON:

EVENING:

NOTES:

Daily Planner

DATE
_____

TOP PRIORITIES:

APPOINTMENTS:

GOALS FOR THE DAY::

MORNING:

AFTERNOON:

EVENING:

NOTES:

Daily Planner

DATE

_____

TOP PRIORITIES:

APPOINTMENTS:

GOALS FOR THE DAY::

MORNING:

AFTERNOON:

EVENING:

NOTES:

Daily Planner

DATE

MORNING:

TOP PRIORITIES:

AFTERNOON:

EVENING:

APPOINTMENTS:

NOTES:

GOALS FOR THE DAY::

Daily Planner

DATE

_____

TOP PRIORITIES:

APPOINTMENTS:

GOALS FOR THE DAY::

MORNING:

AFTERNOON:

EVENING:

NOTES:

Weekly Snapshot

MON:

TUE:

WED:

THUR:

FRI:

SAT:

SUN:

TO DO LIST

NOTES

REMINDERS

My Action Plan

DATE:

TOP PRIORITIES   GOALS

ACTION STEPS   STATUS   ✓

MILESTONES & REWARDS:

THOUGHTS & REFLECTIONS::

Weekly Priority List

MON	
TUE	
WED	
THUR	
FRI	
SAT	
SUN	

Checklist

FOR: DATE:

NOTES:

Daily Planner

DATE

TOP PRIORITIES:

APPOINTMENTS:

GOALS FOR THE DAY::

MORNING:

AFTERNOON:

EVENING:

NOTES:

Daily Planner

DATE
_____

MORNING:

TOP PRIORITIES:

AFTERNOON:

EVENING:

APPOINTMENTS:

NOTES:

GOALS FOR THE DAY::

Daily Planner

DATE

_____

MORNING:

TOP PRIORITIES:

AFTERNOON:

EVENING:

APPOINTMENTS:

NOTES:

GOALS FOR THE DAY::

Daily Planner

DATE

_____

TOP PRIORITIES:

APPOINTMENTS:

GOALS FOR THE DAY::

MORNING:

AFTERNOON:

EVENING:

NOTES:

Daily Planner

DATE

MORNING:

TOP PRIORITIES:

AFTERNOON:

APPOINTMENTS:

EVENING:

NOTES:

GOALS FOR THE DAY::

Daily Planner

DATE

_____

TOP PRIORITIES:

APPOINTMENTS:

GOALS FOR THE DAY::

MORNING:

AFTERNOON:

EVENING:

NOTES:

Daily Planner

DATE

_____

TOP PRIORITIES:

APPOINTMENTS:

GOALS FOR THE DAY::

MORNING:

AFTERNOON:

EVENING:

NOTES:

Weekly Snapshot

MON:

TUE:

WED:

THUR:

FRI:

SAT:

SUN:

REMINDERS

TO DO LIST

NOTES

My Action Plan

DATE:

TOP PRIORITIES

GOALS

ACTION STEPS

STATUS   ✓

MILESTONES & REWARDS:

THOUGHTS & REFLECTIONS::

Weekly Priority List

MON

TUE

WED

THUR

FRI

SAT

SUN

Checklist

FOR: DATE: ✓

NOTES:

Daily Planner

DATE

_____

MORNING:

TOP PRIORITIES:

AFTERNOON:

EVENING:

APPOINTMENTS:

NOTES:

GOALS FOR THE DAY::

Daily Planner

DATE
_____

TOP PRIORITIES:

APPOINTMENTS:

GOALS FOR THE DAY::

MORNING:

AFTERNOON:

EVENING:

NOTES:

Daily Planner

DATE
_____

TOP PRIORITIES:

APPOINTMENTS:

GOALS FOR THE DAY::

MORNING:

AFTERNOON:

EVENING:

NOTES:

Daily Planner

DATE

TOP PRIORITIES:

APPOINTMENTS:

GOALS FOR THE DAY::

MORNING:

AFTERNOON:

EVENING:

NOTES:

Daily Planner

DATE
_____

TOP PRIORITIES:

APPOINTMENTS:

GOALS FOR THE DAY::

MORNING:

AFTERNOON:

EVENING:

NOTES:

Daily Planner

DATE

TOP PRIORITIES:

APPOINTMENTS:

GOALS FOR THE DAY::

MORNING:

AFTERNOON:

EVENING:

NOTES:

Daily Planner

DATE

_____

TOP PRIORITIES:

APPOINTMENTS:

GOALS FOR THE DAY::

MORNING:

AFTERNOON:

EVENING:

NOTES:

Weekly Snapshot

MON:

TUE:

WED:

THUR:

FRI:

SAT:

SUN:

TO DO LIST

NOTES

REMINDERS

My Action Plan

DATE:

TOP PRIORITIES   GOALS

ACTION STEPS   STATUS   ✓

MILESTONES & REWARDS:

THOUGHTS & REFLECTIONS::

Weekly Priority List

MON	
TUE	
WED	
THUR	
FRI	
SAT	
SUN	

Checklist

FOR: DATE:

NOTES:

Daily Planner

DATE
_____

MORNING:

TOP PRIORITIES:

AFTERNOON:

EVENING:

APPOINTMENTS:

NOTES:

GOALS FOR THE DAY::

Daily Planner

DATE
_____

TOP PRIORITIES:

APPOINTMENTS:

GOALS FOR THE DAY::

MORNING:

AFTERNOON:

EVENING:

NOTES:

Daily Planner

DATE

TOP PRIORITIES:

APPOINTMENTS:

GOALS FOR THE DAY::

MORNING:

AFTERNOON:

EVENING:

NOTES:

Daily Planner

DATE

_____

TOP PRIORITIES:

APPOINTMENTS:

GOALS FOR THE DAY::

MORNING:

AFTERNOON:

EVENING:

NOTES:

Daily Planner

DATE
_____

TOP PRIORITIES:

APPOINTMENTS:

GOALS FOR THE DAY::

MORNING:

AFTERNOON:

EVENING:

NOTES:

Daily Planner

DATE
_____

MORNING:

TOP PRIORITIES:

AFTERNOON:

EVENING:

APPOINTMENTS:

NOTES:

GOALS FOR THE DAY::

Daily Planner

DATE

MORNING:

TOP PRIORITIES:

AFTERNOON:

EVENING:

APPOINTMENTS:

NOTES:

GOALS FOR THE DAY::

Weekly Snapshot

MON:

TUE:

WED:

THUR:

FRI:

SAT:

SUN:

REMINDERS

TO DO LIST

NOTES

My Action Plan

DATE:

TOP PRIORITIES

GOALS

ACTION STEPS   STATUS   ✓

MILESTONES & REWARDS:

THOUGHTS & REFLECTIONS::

Weekly Priority List

MON

TUE

WED

THUR

FRI

SAT

SUN

Checklist

FOR: DATE: ✓

NOTES:

Daily Planner

DATE
_____

TOP PRIORITIES:

APPOINTMENTS:

GOALS FOR THE DAY::

MORNING:

AFTERNOON:

EVENING:

NOTES:

Daily Planner

DATE

TOP PRIORITIES:

APPOINTMENTS:

GOALS FOR THE DAY::

MORNING:

AFTERNOON:

EVENING:

NOTES:

Daily Planner

DATE
_____

TOP PRIORITIES:

APPOINTMENTS:

MORNING:

AFTERNOON:

EVENING:

NOTES:

GOALS FOR THE DAY::

Daily Planner

DATE

TOP PRIORITIES:

APPOINTMENTS:

GOALS FOR THE DAY::

MORNING:

AFTERNOON:

EVENING:

NOTES:

Daily Planner

DATE
_____

TOP PRIORITIES:

APPOINTMENTS:

GOALS FOR THE DAY::

MORNING:

AFTERNOON:

EVENING:

NOTES:

Daily Planner

DATE

_____

TOP PRIORITIES:

APPOINTMENTS:

GOALS FOR THE DAY::

MORNING:

AFTERNOON:

EVENING:

NOTES:

Daily Planner

DATE
_____

TOP PRIORITIES:

APPOINTMENTS:

MORNING:

AFTERNOON:

EVENING:

NOTES:

GOALS FOR THE DAY::

Weekly Snapshot

MON:

TUE:

WED:

THUR:

FRI:

SAT:

SUN:

TO DO LIST

NOTES

REMINDERS

My Action Plan

DATE:

TOP PRIORITIES   GOALS

ACTION STEPS   STATUS   ✓

MILESTONES & REWARDS:

THOUGHTS & REFLECTIONS::

Weekly Priority List

MON	
TUE	
WED	
THUR	
FRI	
SAT	
SUN	

Checklist

FOR: DATE:

NOTES:

Daily Planner

DATE

_____

TOP PRIORITIES:

MORNING:

AFTERNOON:

EVENING:

APPOINTMENTS:

NOTES:

GOALS FOR THE DAY::

Daily Planner

DATE

_____

TOP PRIORITIES:

MORNING:

AFTERNOON:

EVENING:

APPOINTMENTS:

NOTES:

GOALS FOR THE DAY::

Daily Planner

DATE

_____

TOP PRIORITIES:

APPOINTMENTS:

GOALS FOR THE DAY::

MORNING:

AFTERNOON:

EVENING:

NOTES:

Daily Planner

DATE

_____

TOP PRIORITIES:

APPOINTMENTS:

GOALS FOR THE DAY::

MORNING:

AFTERNOON:

EVENING:

NOTES:

Daily Planner

DATE

TOP PRIORITIES:

APPOINTMENTS:

GOALS FOR THE DAY::

MORNING:

AFTERNOON:

EVENING:

NOTES:

Daily Planner

DATE

_____

TOP PRIORITIES:

MORNING:

AFTERNOON:

EVENING:

APPOINTMENTS:

NOTES:

GOALS FOR THE DAY::

Daily Planner

DATE

TOP PRIORITIES:

APPOINTMENTS:

GOALS FOR THE DAY::

MORNING:

AFTERNOON:

EVENING:

NOTES:

Weekly Snapshot

MON:

TUE:

WED:

THUR:

FRI:

SAT:

SUN:

REMINDERS

TO DO LIST

NOTES

My Action Plan

DATE:

TOP PRIORITIES

GOALS

ACTION STEPS

STATUS ✓

MILESTONES & REWARDS:

THOUGHTS & REFLECTIONS::

Weekly Priority List

MON

TUE

WED

THUR

FRI

SAT

SUN

Checklist

FOR: DATE:

NOTES:

Daily Planner

DATE

_____

TOP PRIORITIES:

APPOINTMENTS:

GOALS FOR THE DAY::

MORNING:

AFTERNOON:

EVENING:

NOTES:

Daily Planner

DATE

TOP PRIORITIES:

APPOINTMENTS:

GOALS FOR THE DAY::

MORNING:

AFTERNOON:

EVENING:

NOTES:

Daily Planner

DATE

_____

TOP PRIORITIES:

APPOINTMENTS:

GOALS FOR THE DAY::

MORNING:

AFTERNOON:

EVENING:

NOTES:

Daily Planner

DATE

MORNING:

TOP PRIORITIES:

AFTERNOON:

EVENING:

APPOINTMENTS:

NOTES:

GOALS FOR THE DAY::

Daily Planner

DATE
_____

TOP PRIORITIES:

APPOINTMENTS:

GOALS FOR THE DAY::

MORNING:

AFTERNOON:

EVENING:

NOTES:

Daily Planner

DATE

TOP PRIORITIES:

APPOINTMENTS:

GOALS FOR THE DAY::

MORNING:

AFTERNOON:

EVENING:

NOTES:

Daily Planner

DATE

_____

TOP PRIORITIES:

APPOINTMENTS:

GOALS FOR THE DAY::

MORNING:

AFTERNOON:

EVENING:

NOTES:

Daily Planner

DATE

TOP PRIORITIES:

APPOINTMENTS:

GOALS FOR THE DAY::

MORNING:

AFTERNOON:

EVENING:

NOTES:

Daily Planner

DATE

_____

TOP PRIORITIES:

APPOINTMENTS:

GOALS FOR THE DAY::

MORNING:

AFTERNOON:

EVENING:

NOTES:

Daily Planner

DATE

_____

TOP PRIORITIES:

APPOINTMENTS:

GOALS FOR THE DAY::

MORNING:

AFTERNOON:

EVENING:

NOTES:

Daily Planner

DATE

_____

TOP PRIORITIES:

APPOINTMENTS:

GOALS FOR THE DAY::

MORNING:

AFTERNOON:

EVENING:

NOTES:

Daily Planner

DATE

MORNING:

TOP PRIORITIES:

AFTERNOON:

EVENING:

APPOINTMENTS:

NOTES:

GOALS FOR THE DAY::